Alynn!
Who can stop any of us from
the swift speeds of words.
Only us ourselves. Why hesitate.
Just...
Jim

Kerosene

KEROSENE

Tim Seibles

Timothy D. Seibles
3-99

&
Ampersand Press/Bristol, RI

ACKNOWLEDGEMENTS

Poems from this manuscript have appeared in the following journals:

Callaloo: "Outtakes from an Interview with Malcolm X," Vol. 16, No. 3 (Summer 1993). The Johns Hopkins University Press. Baltimore.
Calliope: "Simon Barsinister," "This Is the Reason," "The Groom"
Hanging Loose: "The Stupid"
Kenyon Review: "Check Outside"
New Texas, a Center for Texas Studies book: "From the Diary of Quai Chang Caine," "Kerosene," "Meditation on a Woman by a Window"
Ploughshares: "Hardie"

composition and design by Ampersand Press

Library of Congress Catolog Card Number: 94-73725
ISBN: 0-935331-16-6
Copyright © 1995 by Tim Seibles

first printing, April 1995
second printing, May 1996

Printed in U.S.A.

Published by Ampersand Press, Creative Writing Program , Roger Williams University, Bristol, RI 02809

CONTENTS

The Herd	7
From the Diary of Quai Chang Caine	10
Hardie	14
The Stupid	17
Latin	19
The Groom	22
Meditation on a Woman by a Window	24
Rush	26
Marrow	27
Simon Barsinister	28
Kerosene	29
Check Outside	30
This is the Reason	32
Outtakes from an Interview with Malcolm X	33
You	39

The Herd

Some of the light, some of the first light
arrived so softly it could have been dew
drawn from the night air, and in the creamy-
blue distance thunderheads flickered.

They were still sleeping then, scattered
under trees or in groups in the open,
their slate-colored flanks lightening.

Overnight three had been killed, but the wild dogs
were gone now and the scavengers too,
and the lake began to show dawn its muddy edges.

What was surprising was that they ever slept
at all—with so many things alive in the dark,
but they slept well, dreaming exactly what they
dreamed they should dream, and when the strongest one
rolled back the silence with a long, throbbing yawn,

the others answered, divvying up the air
with staccato croaks, shrill bleats and near-
growls—some with front legs still bent
under them, some with eyes caught shining
as if they had never before seen the world.

No one knew how long they had been here
or what to call them   or how it was that they came
to understand themselves, what to do, where to go.

But they moved together like a slow wind,
as a wind moves from one place to another,
dying off but rising again, the same wind moving.

And when the must broke into their blood
they coupled fiercely, almost in a panic, as if

one by one they were beginning to drown—the heat
sliding over each in turn like the shadow of a cloud.

* * * * *

Once it had cleared the treetops, the sun paved
the veldt bright yellow, and the stilt-legged birds
that had been chitter-whistling since early early,
quieted; some stood in the shallows
stabbing the lake for lazy, flat-headed fish.

The herd was eating too, nudging each other for room,
nostrils flexing wet and open. You might have
thought they'd been made for nothing but
filling their mouths, so content did they seem
tugging at the stringy greens with their square teeth.

They were not stupid; though sometimes when weather
changed unexpectedly, they would simply stampede
barrel-eyed while the rain snapped against their backs.
And if one among them bore some odd marking,
when it reached a certain age, the others
drove it away with head-butts and hard kicks.

I saw it happen once: a female with a bronze-colored face
instead of the usual gray, limped a short ways
behind the herd, her right foreleg fractured.
Each time she tried to rejoin they attacked—mainly
the bulls and ranking cows—stomping, frothing,
fussing up immense heaves of dust.

The wounded animal seemed confused, not seeing, not
being able to see what was wrong, unable to keep
from following, just as the attackers couldn't
stop themselves, couldn't understand what stranged
inside their skulls to turn them against their own.

* * * * *

The dogs were made for this—
their sharp, felt-furred ears barely visible
gliding above the high weeds by the lake,
and when they took the open field their feet
kissed the earth for allowing such speed
and the taste of meat and they were upon her
and the air turned over, so heavy with the smell
of blood, it was nearly animal itself.

Hard to say what went on inside the herd
with death blossoming right there,
or if any had actually watched the kill,
or if it made a difference either way.
The dogs would always be there
blind but for their teeth, and the herd
would continue to find the sunrise
next to the dark, returning from sleep
to offer their young to the flat world.

And was it anything like sorrow
that brought a few back days later
to scuff the ground where that one
with the new face had fallen?

Or just some dumb itch of memory,
some lizard's blink of deja-vu,
the future circling
to take them along.

From The Diary
Of Quai Chang Caine, Shaolin Monk

found in 1883 near
McGehee, TX

My life, explained to flies, would have them laughing.

Two years ago I killed the Emperor's oldest son.

On the holy road to the Temple of Heaven
I buried a spear in his back
because one of the Royal Guard killed my old teacher, Po.

He had stumbled in front of the Prince's caravan.

A good man lost because those with power
have no time for those without it.

And it must be a strange pleasure   believing the world
was made only for you, that your wealth is proof,
that the breeze actually prefers your face.

I thought I would die in China that day—

with the large bounty offered by the Royal House
and the random hangings—

but the people kept my shadow in their pockets.

I have the robes that say I know
killing does no one honor,
that no injury is ever rightly avenged.

But what do I do with the ache in my blood
that was eased when I threw the spear?

February 1881
aboard cargo ship,
"Yun Hee"

* * * * *

Now, I am in Mescalero, New Mexico—America—a half-white
    Shaolin,
always only a few steps ahead of the price for my death.

Mostly, people here are hard-working and stupid.
If an American has two thoughts the first and the second involve
    money.

Though skin lies simply along the surface of a man,
people here think it is a sign of something deep—grace
if you are white   fault if you are not.

There are places where I can not get a glass of water.

By my eyes they know I am not white, but by my height and color
they suspect I am not *not white*.

October 1881
Carrizozo, NM

* * * * *

Yesterday, I blinded someone
for spitting on my food. He laughed.
Then I reached into his face. It happened
so quickly—I swear, for that second,
my hand belonged to someone else.

* * * * *

I have seen black people and red also and others not seen in China.

To witness hate coming to live along the lines of skin—
suppose some rabid animal were roaming the countryside,
everyone would agree to kill it, to stop it somehow. Here,

it is as if people would take this thing in and feed it,
so quick they are to nurse this cruelty.

January 1882
Kenna, NM

* * * * *

It is unfortunate that the whites here are so many.
They have grown invisible to themselves   like the air
which is also everywhere.

In a hundred years
much will be regretted and very little forgiven.

May 1882
Paducah, TX

* * * * *

There is a woman named Qi Do.
Two eyes are not enough to hold the shimmer in her hair.
Some days I catch my heart trying to memorize her face.

A man, the sheriff's friend, tried to open her blouse.
I merely turned his hand and told him she was not
from the saloon.

He said he would peel me "like a slant-eyed banana."

When I killed the Prince, I became sick in my stomach,
though the Royal House is yet famous for torture.

When I killed the assassin sent after me, it was like
slapping a mosquito poised to suck from my wrist.

Laotzu has written, "One who recognizes all men
as members of his own body
is a sound man to guard them."

I am a priest. I believe in living
toward this. But often my anger occurs to me

as its own creature   with its own teeth.

* * * * *

> July 1882
> Knox City, TX

To those who would sleep through the wounds
they inflict on others,
I offer pain to help them awaken, maybe death to keep them calm.

There is no question injustice can ask
to which violence is not a fair answer.

The man who wanted to peel me—I helped him
fit half his blade into his thigh,
his right hand still on the hilt.

The look on his face then:
as if he had seen a sparrow swallowing a wolf.

* * * * *

> November 1882
> Abilene, TX

All my life I have stood apart from other Chinese
because I looked white, and here   been outcast by whites
for the shape of my eyes. Now I see beauty
in the motions of revenge, the making of harm—

so now   I am not even Shaolin.

But why should belonging be such a prize?
Except to one who needs others
to tell him his name.

Membership is only another word for obedience.
Obedience is for dogs and children.

I know who I am   but where can I live?

Hardie

You know how tiny kids walk up to you, raise their arms
and expect to be picked up—I used to do that; that was me.

Me, with my diaper full and my nose half crusty.

I remember being eye to eye with the little doors
underneath the kitchen sink—I was a child, seriously.

I used to yank open those cabinets and see the shiny colors
and glass: the orange box of Tide, the pink bottle leaking
dishwashing liquid, a green Pine Sol thing with big yellow letters.

Of course, I couldn't read and before I could touch anything
my mom was snatching me back, slapping my hands—

that shit hurt! My hands were really little, really
new, like shoots fresh out of the ground,
really soft—I was a child. Is that clear?

People just put me to bed whenever they felt like it.
People sat me on the potty every other whenever
and said *Go!*

I didn't have any words, just sloppy, muddy kinds of garbled
    clucks
that wanted to be words, that tried to be wordish—

Think of the amount of criticism I got. Criticism piled on
like cold cream of wheat.

It was like I couldn't do anything right—not a goddamn thing!

Picture *me* in a high chair being pressured to eat—
they might have been dangling a secret agent off a cliff
trying to make him give up something top-secret—

I was little; my legs hardly held me up; everybody
stood around poised to catch me—
Ooops! Oooopsy! Whoops-a-daisy!

How could I get my confidence?

But now I'm big, I eat ice cream all the time—I'm big; I use
the *Men's* room; nobody tells me what to do,

even though I feel like I'm holding onto my life the way a
wounded ant clings to a window screen. I'm

big now. Big and musty. Big enough to hide my baby shoes
in the palm of one hand.

But once I was a kid. I didn't
need deodorants. I sat on my grandmother's lap
and ate candy spearmint leaves.

I wasn't down on white people. I
didn't even know I was black. My whole bag
was cartoons—I was a child, goddammit!

Just a mouthful of Tonka Toys and Lego,
a little guy with no sense of time passing.
Where was everybody going? What happened to *Johnny Quest?!*

Next thing I know, I got this *hardie* thumping around
on my belly—every morning, fearless, like
my own bad-ass rooster—sun-up and *cock-a-doodle-doo!*

I couldn't pee with it and nobody would tell me what it was for.

I wasn't always so worldly. I wasn't always a madman
over women's legs, either. I spent my first fifteen years
without a real kiss.

I was a child. You think I don't remember?!
You think it's easy keeping all this innocence pent up inside?!

And now, when it comes to money, I'm like some dizzy insect
full of wanting it, like some big bluebottle fly
tipsy over a mound of shit.

I wasn't always like this.

Parts of me started getting large, growing hair:
my underarms, my wrists, even the tops of my feet.

But I *was* a little boy once: really curious, really small, really scared—

Is that clear?

The Stupid

I no longer know what it means.
I no longer know what to say about
anything that has anything
to do with anything—not that
anyone else has ever really known ever
before either, but I hold the record
for consecutive days totally dumbfounded.
Watch this: See what I mean?
It's in my eyes—I am ignorant of
everything to a very large degree—
to a degree so large in fact that
if this degree were a fly swatter
you could smash all of Philadelphia with it,
or if this degree were a planet   it'd be
Jupiter. See what I mean? Nobody should even
talk to me, not even a nervous hello
from someone white passing me on the street,
not even a sidelong growl from some
mange-ravaged mutt named Mortimer,
not with all this stupid I've got piled up
inside. I no longer know
what it means—know what I mean?
I wake up all excited and can't remember
what was what in my dreams. I let
somebody take my pulse and now
I need the damn thing—to locate my

wrists, just to find my hands. Last week
I picked up an encyclopedia, you know,
trying to find a cure, and the sucker
shriveled up like a cold prune's penis.
That's what a bad case of stupid can do.
Somebody starts a war—next thing you know
you're tying yellow ribbons on everything.
Once, after the riot, I saw the President
sound-biting about what caused the thing
in L.A., about how it had nothing to do
with race, and I knew, for certain, the stupid
had made a mess of him. Now it's me—
one telethon won't do it, not ten probably
either, but research is a start I guess.
I just wish I knew where I caught it.
Ask me anything about America: See what I mean?

Latin

Words slip into a language the way
white-green shoots slide between slats in a fence.

A couple opens the door to a restaurant,
sees the orange and black colors everywhere

and the waitress grins, "Yeah,
a little Halloween overkill, huh."

Overkill, a noun for all of us
fidgeting under the nuclear umbrella—

but for that instant it just meant too many decorations,
too many paper skeletons and hobgobbled balloons.

* * * * *

I know a woman who is tall with dark hair,
who makes me think of honeysuckle

whenever she opens her legs. Not just the flower
but the dew-soaked music itself *honeysuckle* like a flavor.

And I remember the first time years back
when LaTina told me what it was we had

between our eight-year-old front teeth
that April afternoon, our hands wet

with rain from the vines. "Honey sickle," she said,
while the white flower bloomed from the side of her mouth,

and I had a new sweetness on my tongue and a word
I'd never heard before. How was it decided in the beginning?

This word   for *this* particular thing,
a sound attached to a shape or a feeling forever.

* * * * *

All summer long the cicadas don't know
what we call them.

They sneak from the ground every year after dark,
break out of their shells right into the language,

and it holds them like a net made of nothing
but the need to make everything familiar.

All summer long they rattle trees like maracas
until they become part of our weather—

quiet in rain, crazy in hard sun,
so we say *those cicadas sure make enough noise, huh.*

And the noise of that sentence   heard ten-thousand times
becomes a name for *us* the cicadas keep trying to say.

* * * * *

I think about dying sometimes,
not the sudden death in the movies—

the red hole in the shirt, the eyes
open like magazines left on a waiting room table—

not that, but withering slowly like a language,
barely holding on until everything

I ever did or said   is just gone, absorbed
into something I would never have imagined—

like Latin. Not lost completely, but moved away
from that bright, small place

between seeing   and naming,
between the slow roll of ocean

and the quick intake of air
that will fill the word *wave*.

The Groom

for Jim Esber & Jane Fine

When I first saw you   I wanted
to talk to you   I wanted to
touch your shoulder   I noticed
how the day had gone dark with clouds
and I noticed   your eyes
darker still   And when I saw you I
wanted to tell you something
about a feeling I had   about you or
possibly because of you   how when I looked
to where you stood talking   my skin
tried to walk away from my bones   toward you
how my bones wanted to go along   When I saw you
glance over grinning from your conversation
I noticed your mouth   the cranberry red
of your lips   and I thought   a kiss I
thought maybe if I could balance
myself against your lips   for awhile
I could keep   from falling   I thought
if you let me kiss you sometime   I would be
happier—I might even be a
better person   When I saw you throw
your head back laughing   both hands
squeezing your hips   I thought about
your body   not something sexual
necessarily   nothing necessarily concerning

sex   the way some thoughts   sometimes
do   but about my hands   landing
somewhere around your knees—softly
as though having just   parachuted from the sky
just above them   I thought about
just walking over
and saying *Come hither, curly-haired maiden,*
the city in my brain is burning,
and the people there cry out
for your mercy   I didn't know
what   you would think of me
How do we ever   cover the ground
between wanting   and having   between
one nervous solitude and another
I didn't know   I still   don't know

I just wanted to ask you   your name I
wanted to tell you   that your eyes
were very brown   that your eyes—
that some evening   I would like to
walk into them   and take you with me

Meditation on a Woman by a Window

for Sarah Boardman

I bet you waited all day for the rain
to bring back your shadow
                          half-whispering
almost singing something, some old
music pooling inside you slowly

as if the melody were calling the words
one by one   from the storm.

You seem sad, even with evening
dressing the wall beside you
                          as though you
want to be touched but at the same time
left alone.
          I almost understand: even when I
close my blinds and unplug the phone

I still think about someone for company

as if all this walking around inside
could conjure an answer to this held breath
that has become my life.
                            Some days I feel myself
falling out of myself
the way night falls into the air.

Other evenings I watch sunset scatter the light
running blood-orange to peach-blue
                            and I want to go
someplace where the weather is the language

where I won't end up staring
at these pages

                        writing toward a love
no one can have.

Wherever you are right now
I believe the hours open like evening
along the bright edge of your body

while outside my door
                        October walks
cool wind into rain and trees
change in whispers.

Rush

Let's slow it   all down
so the sparrows   sound like bullfrogs
and the bullfrogs   low like cattle
and the cows   become four-legged tubas
and the tubas   play the music
redwoods make   when they groove
long roots   into earth

And this afternoon   around 4 o'clock
the second-hand   will be   almost asleep
the tick   so far   from the tock
they could be   two whales   in two separate seas
and when you come   at that hour
with someone's mouth   like sangria

it will last   for weeks   one
slow gasp   after another   after
the next   your heart   like the lazy giant
chasing Jack   stealing the goose
with the golden eggs   Fe
Fi   Fo
Fum

Marrow

I suppose it is too late to say there is a lesson
in the way a woman's eyes take over an evening,
how her legs move all the tall ships in my blood—

and this thread pulled taut around my belly,
the liquid spool of her hips finding the book of praise
inside me; how old must I get not to feel it

opening like a door in my chest. Inside me
there must be an abandoned city where only
one man lives walking around looking for company,

while inside him someone else calls out
in some other solitary place. To the marrow,
I think this keeps being true.

I have opened my eyes every day for 38 years
and I am not much wiser, no matter how it all pours in,
but so often and unslowly the world is simply the face

and fluid gait of a woman coming into view.
I can't say anything else about it: these open streets
and lamplit avenues; the beautiful names gathering

along the tongue's front edge, a surge of something
like a prayer   for someone to touch, loneliness,
my lungs almost holding onto the air—her mouth
delicious, her legs, one moving next to the other.

Simon Barsinister:
Simon Says, "Go Snow"

So much rain in their goodie-goodie hearts—
so many sad sighs, so much grinding in their flimsy, little guts.
And *oh, if only this* and *boohoo, why that*—
as if anybody could ever turn back these headlines.

One thing Underdog always forgets: evil is easy.
Evil invents. Evil can make something out of nothing—
and there's always plenty of that.

What does a hero **do** these days anyway—
pull kitty-kats out of big trees, snatch a baby
out of a burning house   back into the world?
Take a little peek outside.

Is this really someplace you   want to be?
Weather doesn't have much to do
with wind and sleet. Not really.

More with that high stupidity that sweats your cities.
(Get it?) If Sweet Polly Purebred lived in Harlem
nobody'd give a damn whether I burned or froze her.
That's the eye of the storm—my favorite season.

Evil is easy. Just keep people believing
what they already do. They'll bring the appropriate
sky. Don't ever talk to strangers.

Read the papers.
It's all my Weather Machine. I flip a switch:
I'm the only game in town. Everywhere.
Help, Underdog! Save me!   Heh-heh-heh.

Kerosene

> *after the L.A. riot,*
> *April '92*

In my country the weather—
it's not too good   At every bus stop anger
holds her umbrella folded her
face buckled tight as a boot   Along the avenues
beneath parked cars spent
cartridges glimmer   A man's head crushed
by nightsticks smoke   still
slides from his mouth   Let out wearing
uniforms hyenas rove in packs
unmuzzled and brothers strain inside
their brown skins like something wounded
thrown into a lake   Slowly
like blood filling
cracks in the street slowly   the
President   arrived   his mouth
slit into his face   Like candles seen
through thick curtains   sometimes
at night the dark citizens occur to him

like fishing lamps along
the black shore of a lake   like moths
soaked in kerosene and lit

Check Outside

They believe that if they remain
frightened enough for long enough
things won't happen.   You know—*things*.

Listen to a city late at night:
the dead-bolts clapped into place,
tv's spitting on the floor, upstairs
mothers hammering Jesus
into their black thumbs.

But things will happen. Even here
with everybody here. People are going
to do some more things. You see it
all the time. Starting now

and from now on, weather is weather,
and news is weather too.
Who do you think is behind
all those uniforms? Your plans:

your ideas   about tomorrow.
Even now, the blood turns
in your ear—a story. You want
a story.

But right now we're right

in the middle of something really
funny, and let me tell you: it's something
like a story, all this.

People with chips—heavy chips
on their shoulders. People with a few
tricks up their sleeves   have
got to do some more.   things.

Check outside—how the wind runs
from some exact somewhere. That man
on the wall by the *A&P*—what's
he got in his hand?

Some people were playing cards... and among the players was a young man who at one point, without saying anything, laid down his cards, left the bar, ran across the deck, and threw himself into the sea. By the time the boat was stopped... the body couldn't be found.

—Marguerite Duras
from *The Lover*

This Is the Reason

This. This white railing. This
something like sorrow,

something like a scraped knee—
but in your brain. This long wait

with whatever's next
like powdered glass on your tongue. This.

These hands. These dead stars
tilling the dark. This ache like ice

on a tooth, only
all the time, like a time you

really needed to say something. This
itching scab in the heart.

This something
like not breathing when

you're breathing. This. This
Pepsi jingle, the newspaper,

these insects, this evening, that cigarette.

Outtakes from an Interview
with Malcolm X after Mecca

January 1965

My going to prison simply made it clear
that I had already been in prison.
If you misinform a man his mind becomes a cage,
and everything he does is just him
reaching a paw between the bars; you get too close,
you get clawed. Next question.

Now, I think you already know what television
means to me: Cowboys   Indians   Bo-Jangles dancing
with that little blond girl   *Tarzan*   and that
damn collie, *Lassie*—white people picture themselves
over and over as the good guys, but look what they've done.

You don't want me to lie, do you? When brown eyes
look into blue eyes—in this country—how
can we not   be shoved up against these last 500 years?

No, America has not been anything like a melting pot
where black people are concerned, but it will be heating up—
    shortly.

Wait. Wait a minute. I **am** absolutely against people mistreating
    people.
It does not matter who   but if you've hurt somebody
for no reason   you've got to expect to get hurt
for *no reason*. That's not radical. That's human.
But these white folks, these Christians   killing and praying
for nothing but profit and some sick dream
of supremacy   and, on top of that, always assuming
the moral high ground—now **that's** radical.
You might even call that   *extreme.*

But you know I'm not writing the history books.
I'm too busy being dangerous   according to the news.
Even though no one has ever seen me hurt anybody.
And the papers can't get finished with all this about
"Hate Monger X" and "X advocates violent revolution."

Let me tell you, don't nobody need to mong any more hate;
brotherhood is the real revolution—in Mecca
I was on my knees beside men of every shade.
But how do you get to brotherhood   **here**
where it's so clear that so many people
need their asses kicked.

I already said white skin won't necessarily make someone evil,
though I know what America has done—to white people—
continues to infect them. And they keep dragging their feet
about getting a cure: if it was obvious that I had
something deadly you could *catch*
wouldn't you be, um, *upset*, if I kept saying
Next week I'll see a doctor. Really, I don't feel
all that bad.
                    And anyone who wants to argue
whether or not Europe and her children
have been a blessing or a plague to the rest of us
doesn't really want to argue at all.
Just let them dig through the rubble; let them
do a body count. Ask Africa   Ask India   Ask Asia
Visit a *reservation.*

Look, what I honestly want to talk about
is unity   and how complicated that is, and how
I'm afraid that my life has been a waste, that maybe,
finally, no one will understand what
I'm trying to do. Black Americans
talk about wanting to get even, but don't know
how to take care of each other first.
And I wish I understood what made whites
want to hurt us so much so badly.

Have you ever seen a man lynched? Ever
walked into a ghetto? If you do you'll see
that nothing but dope is keeping a lot of brothers
from chewing off their own hands.

Suppose you were outnumbered and surrounded
by some kind of relentless carnivore
that could come get you anytime, could
snatch you up without even mustering a thought—
and it *is* like that—what would happen
to your mind? Wouldn't you start killing
yourself   rather than waiting to be eaten
alive?
         Black on black crime is
a form of suicide. Gangs, drugs—
they're all part of a community trying
to slit its own wrists. Nobody
wants to deal with this. Sociologists say
build more recreation centers,
Give The Negro More Basketballs,
as if our true home was a gym.

The question is   how do you teach people
who have been taught that they have no value
to love themselves   when even the act of learning
is an act of self-love?

Really, underneath all this talking I do
is just a cry for help from a man close to drowning—
I mean we're all choking on this thing, brother—
America is already underwater.

Sometimes, you're right, sometimes rage
told me what to say, and I meant it   **in my bones.**
But you can't build a bridge out of fire—
I know that now—and you can't take the hand
of a man whose back is to you

                    and how do you
forgive someone who feels no need to apologize?

I know King worries about this. Jesus
or no Jesus, it **must** drive him crazy sometimes.

You honestly believe Dr. King never dreams
of using his fist?

And you think I *enjoy* being angry? I don't.
Nobody was born to be angry.
                    And maybe I
have been foolish. I wanted a place to stand
that would stay beneath my feet. I thought The Nation
of Islam was that place. I believed Elijah Muhammad
had the map, that if I could hold myself steady,
face forward, not blinking, shoes polished and pointed
his way, I would walk right out of this insane,
racist shit   right into the truth—

or maybe the truth would find me, the way
a swollen river claims an insect
and carries it to the water's end.
                    And maybe
that's exactly what happened to me:
once upon a time, I conked my hair, zooted
my suits, smoked reefer   even pimped a little.

Only Allah knows why I didn't die a burglar,
and what it is I've actually become.
And Betty, my wife—I wonder what she sees
when she thinks about *Malcolm X*.
Love? A packed suitcase? A flash
of teeth and glasses as I turn toward the door?

You know what? I'm sick of talking about race—
like I can't have anything else on my mind.

Have you ever seen first dark lie down
across a lake   and what about some nights
some slow jazz sipped straight from the radio?
I want to talk about things worthy of praise—
the fact that somewhere underneath all these colors
we are capable of saying *yes* to each other.

Your newspapers just want a boogie man
to slap on the front page. I want to talk about
what is sacred, how in the Holy Land I pulled
the breath of Allah into my own lungs, how this
made me want to laugh and embrace anyone,
how I want my people to know their skin
unbruised as it had been once
early in the world.

                But History
is moving on like an old bear
with **all** of us in its belly, and most days,
I sense that it's too late—
my life is shrugging me off,
and there's nothing I can do to explain, to
get it back, nothing I can do to get back
inside it. I get phone calls. I get letters.
People want to kill me: my once beloved
Fruit of Islam   and white people,
maybe FBI.
           For all I know
someone white could pay someone
black to do it   or the reverse.

I'm not so afraid of dying,
but if it were up to me I'd sure try
to live a little while more.
I'd like to live long enough to see
my people sharing books like they do barbecue
or beer—especially the young brothers.

All these big fantasies and hard plans
about spilling my blood—why? What
will change   when I'm gone? Who's gonna have
such a good time?

               It's like
I'm on this long street with no intersections.
I'm ready to make a turn, but somebody
keeps taking the corners away—
like in a dream: something bad is after you,
and you're trying to get home,
but your legs are drunk, and you know
it's gaining ground, and when you, just
in the nick of time, touch your door,
it's   not your door   and you know
what's behind you, so somehow you snatch
open you eyes   and, even though
you're sweating in the pitch dark,
you know you're all right, that whatever it was,
it can't reach you, not as long as you
stay awake.   So, what I wish you'd tell me now
is how I can open my eyes
to get out of *this*.

You

are not forgiven
no matter what you say

you are not   you are not   no matter what

The way a man is followed by his shadow, like a three-legged stray,
down all the afternoon streets

so you are followed by our blood
smeared across your teeth

And we are throwing our heads back
dancing still and anyway and almost completely

without you   and your innocence
and your good shoes

No matter when you arrived it was better
before then   though the words you brought for us
are now inside us

Sometimes I look   and a crowd has   gathered   laughing
at someone tied to a tree   and both his arms
are broken   and his clothes are soaked in gasoline

and though it helps
no one now   forgives nothing   now—not at all

I believe it could have been different
I believe you did not think it through

what you were doing   how the others,
those to whom it was done,

might feel about it later
and how difficult   those feelings might be

But maybe *that's tough* as you might say

maybe *that's just too bad*

Tim Seibles was born in Philadelphia in 1955. He moved to Dallas in 1973 to attend Southern Methodist University and remained in Texas teaching high school English for ten years. He received his MFA in Writing from Vermont College in 1990. That same year he was awarded a National Endowment for the Arts grant. In 1991 Tim received a writing fellowship from the Fine Arts Work Center in Provincetown, Massachusetts which brought him to Cape Cod for seven months. He has published two other books of poetry, *Body Moves* and *Hurdy-Gurdy*.